Your MIGHTY *Soul*

12/1/16
To Victoria,
my dear soul-
friend, profound
blessings of peace,
+ grace to you!
love, Molly

Your **MIGHTY** *Soul*

THE BUMPY *and* BEAUTIFUL

ROAD TO YOUR BEST SELF

Molly Glenn

Sacred
Shore
A Sacred Shore LLC Book

A Sacred Shore LLC Book

ISBN 978-0-9968241-0-1

Book design by Ann Lowe

For inquiries contact:

SACRED SHORE LLC
P.O. Box 152889
Austin, TX 78715-2889
www.sacredshore.com

To my beloveds, Jon and Kristen,
your mighty souls are bright lights in this world.

ACKNOWLEDGMENTS

I'm humbly indebted to Spirit for showing me the way to the soul and inspiring every part of this book.

To my husband Jon, you provided the opportunity for me to write, and I'm so grateful for you.

To Kristen, your words of encouragement always lifted me up. You knew I could finish the book.

For Jennifer Hager, my editor, you've been a precious godsend. Your editing skills and intuitive sense have made all the difference.

Heartfelt thanks to dear friends and supporters, especially Dr. Bob Lively and Janet Woodrome. Both of you live the true spirit of love. Also, Amanda Buckalew, Jeri Kramer, Donna Shea LeBlanc, Inga Grunden, Stephanie Barko, Holly Bell, Wendy Gainan, Margie Jackson, Donna Hartley Lucas, Annette Morgan, and Zenith Rose, your lasting friendship has been a marvelous gift to me.

CONTENTS

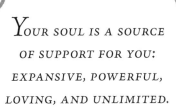

YOUR SOUL IS A SOURCE
OF SUPPORT FOR YOU:
EXPANSIVE, POWERFUL,
LOVING, AND UNLIMITED.

Molly Glenn

Introduction

THIS SMALL BOOK is about a big journey of realization. It's a story of spiritual growth fueled by a belief that each of us *has* a mighty soul and *is* a mighty soul. To be mighty is to be bold and powerful. When we realize this in our deepest self, we begin to blossom.

Coming to this understanding wasn't easy for me. For the longest time, I knew something wasn't right. There was a disconnect between what I expected life to be—how people would act and what I would have and accomplish—and reality. I looked okay on the outside, but I was perpetually unsettled. My faith only took me so far. There had to be a better way to live.

The challenge for me has been learning to accept the messy uncertainties of life. Perhaps that's a challenge for all of us. How there are no guarantees that we'll get what we want. Or that prayers will be answered to our liking. And another: that what we see is only an inkling of what's going on in the greater whole around us. The paradox is to know these limitations and to *find wholeness and balance and peace anyway.*

Your Mighty Soul is a spiritual self-help primer, a how-to for elevating your soul to the forefront of life. Divine presence, love, and insight are available to everyone at any time. This book can help you attune to it. A number of different paths could take you there. I recommend this route because it worked for me.

Spiritual growth widens our perspectives. The ways my own spiritual eyes were opened are woven throughout the book. Dozens of exercises will encourage you to practice new approaches. I'll invite you to write about your experiences in a journal and to learn about stillness. Stories from your past will have much to reveal about you and your relationships.

Exploring your inner landscape in the ways I suggest will take some work. But what an adventure! You'll discover aspects of yourself that surprise and delight you. The world has a sparkle to it you may not have seen before. As you connect to your deepest self and to God, you will know peace. Welcome to a marvelous journey of love and growth.

Molly Glenn
October 2015

WE MUST LEARN TO
REAWAKEN AND KEEP
OURSELVES AWAKE.

Henry David Thoreau,
Walden Pond

Waking Up

THE FIRST TIME I SAW my husband do it, I was curious. We were in our small orchard when he, an arborist, grabbed the trunk of a plum sapling and shook it. The tree had an undersized canopy and was clearly declining. My husband repeated the shaking motions two more times while conveying a mental message: *Wake up. Grow and be strong.* Apparently, old-time gardeners used to jump-start plants in this way.

His technique made sense to me. Vigorous movement combined with intent could awaken the plant's natural impetus to grow. Many of us can be like that stunted plum tree. Cocooning, on permanent hold, stalled out. We feel empty inside and unfulfilled, unable to move forward.

Then something comes along that shakes us from our slumber. It could be a crisis, such as the loss of a loved one or a career. Perhaps it's a gradual buildup of frustration and stress that gets our attention. Positive things can also call us to awaken, such as when an amazing opportunity drops into our lap. Either way, there's a choice—ignore the opportunity or let yourself go in a new direction.

The key is how ready we are to embrace change. We have to feel ready, or at least brave, in order to take action. If you've ever tried to wake someone up who wasn't willing to get going, you know what I mean. You can apply pressure like my husband did, but readiness controls the outcome.

In a spiritual sense, wakefulness is a state of being peacefully alert and self-aware. You're aligned with what you perceive to be the divine flow for your life. As much as you can, you live and breathe, talk and walk, from the most sacred part of yourself.

I'll give you an example of what this can look like. An accomplished young woman, we'll call her Kate, works in human resources for an international company. Not long ago, she described a typical day to me.

She arrives at work early, and the first thing she does is get quiet for about five minutes. Her day will be very busy, so she breathes and relaxes. Kate reminds herself to be open to the circumstances that come, to listen more than she speaks. She vows to keep her attention in the present moment throughout the day. That way, her mind won't be keyed up, trying to solve a stack of problems by the fifth meeting or phone call. This effort helps preserve her physical energy and calm.

There's an ease in not pushing herself to have immediate solutions. She finds that insights come to her more organically now—in the midst of her stillness and presence, listening and being open, and sitting with matters for a bit longer. Spirit has become her guiding force, partnering with her mind as a helpmate and source of wisdom.

Working in this way hasn't been automatic for Kate. We had talked a lot during a shake-up at a previous employer; it had been traumatic for her. Now she's put her backbone and strong desire for success into changing her work habits—choosing attitudes that nourish rather than drain her. For the first time in her life, Kate has a job that's immensely satisfying to her.

Waking up spiritually involves refocusing our attention away from whatever has held it hostage. As with any skill, practice is important. Through practice, we'll find that our wisest self—our soul—is in charge more often. Its vast wisdom becomes accessible to us, as well as peace of mind and body. With such beautiful possibilities emerging, we're poised to take the next step.

~~~~~ GUIDED PRACTICE ~~~~~

I invite you to purchase a journal for your work in this book. It'll be a dedicated place for writing down your observations during the guided practices. You may find that your mind resists doing the writing portion. I suggest that you thank your mind for this feedback and do the written responses anyway, even if it feels awkward at times. A journey of the soul has many steps; documenting your progress can be most helpful.

In a quiet place, open your new journal and date the page. Jot down the questions in the next paragraph. Allow yourself plenty of room for writing your responses, including space for observations that might come later on. Also, a different question may come to your mind than the ones listed. Trust yourself to explore it in detail.

- Begin by scanning the events of your life so far. What instances come to mind that seem to have been wake-up calls? Could these events have been points where you were primed to grow as a person? Describe them.
- Identify a time when you felt fully awake and open. Describe how this felt physically, emotionally, and spiritually.
- On a scale of 1 to 10 (1 being "least" and 10 being "most"), how close in touch do you feel with your deepest self? Add any thoughts.

ETERNAL DIVINE SELF

I'm asking you to get acquainted with your soul in our work together, but what is the soul exactly? Theologians and philosophers have concerned themselves with this for centuries. From study and experience, I know what I can understand (keeping it simple) and what seems correct *for me*. I'm glad to share my thoughts with you.

The idea here is not to promote any religious beliefs over others. We could argue which doctrine is right or wrong until the cows come home. A better route is for you to uncover your own soul and live, truly live, from that sacred place. Then you can practice the religion or philosophy that suits you, its source (and yours) being profound goodness.

My belief is that each one of us is a unique creation arising from divine intelligence. There's no one and no thing just like you. Isn't that something? If you've ever felt low self-esteem as I once did, it is invaluable to realize that belief is false. The truth is that you are precious beyond measure.

Your soul is the center of your being. It's your eternal, divine self, the true essence of who you are. Soul is the animating force in life. It enlivens your physical and mental self. The spark of the Creator comes through your soul (and your DNA). It's how God can be within you and you can be in God at all times.

Soul is a spiritual communication hub, a power center not bound by time and space. Through it, you can know a kinship with people all over the world, past and present. Historical figures, artists, spiritual leaders, authors, relatives, and friends—all can be a rich source of meaning for you.

The natural world is one of the ways we connect to our soul. Nature partners with our soul to elevate us to higher spiritual ground. We sense this when we feel truly at home in a place, whether it's our own garden or an island paradise. Within us there's a sense of belonging and deep appreciation.

If what I'm claiming is new to you, spend some time with the possibility. In quiet moments, *allow your soul to be unlimited.* Give it permission to be what it is without your mind interfering. That's the invitation of this book—to open to your soul and experience its magnificence.

Where does this wonderful soul of ours reside? I feel my sacred center throughout my chest and abdomen, although I'm pretty sure it's not in a fixed place. Think of your soul as being located in the middle of your deepest self. Be sure to include the area around your heart.

Many people believe that the soul is everlasting. When you're born, it accompanies your physical body. At the end of earthly life, your soul provides transportation to the next realm. In any case, you can be comforted in knowing that your soul doesn't leave you because, with a nod to Dr. Seuss, it's the "you-est" you there is.

GUIDED PRACTICE

We could spend a lot of time parsing words and concocting definitions for the soul. But what's important is for you to begin to know this part of yourself—intimately.

This exercise requires you to be in a quiet spot where you'll be uninterrupted. Choose a place where you feel uplifted. The area around you should be uncluttered and have a peaceful vibe. Allow several minutes to complete the exercise.

Sit in a comfortable chair. Begin to imagine the spark of life within you. Perhaps you sense it to be deep in the center of your body. Close your eyes and relax. Think of your soul as the most real and true part of you. In imagining this, what do you see? Any colors or shapes? What do you feel? What thoughts come to mind? Do you feel an aliveness, a pulsing, a quietness, or something else? Spend a few moments in close communion with this part of you.

After you finish this exercise, take time to reconnect with your physical self. Breathe, open your eyes, look around the room, tap your feet on the floor, and wiggle your hands. Wait until you feel alert before standing up. Then consider these questions:

- You used your imagination just now. How real was that experience for you?
- How did your mind accept what you experienced? Did it have something to say about your "visit"?

Make notes in your journal about your experience.

CALL TO CONSCIOUSNESS

Many people would agree that everyone has a soul. And some are convinced that animals have souls. I used to look in my sweet dog's eyes and swear that I could see hers. Indigenous people are said to perceive Spirit all around them in rocks, trees, animals, and other humans. To me, they're ahead of the rest of us in linking consciousness and the soul.

Our soul is this enormous, sacred asset within us. Yet, how much have we invested in getting to know something about our own?

If you're like me, you've read a lot of books. And you may have prayed and perhaps attended church services and/or study groups. These can be lovely ways of being in communion with Spirit and other people. In my case, though, something continued to be missing. It confounded me for the longest time.

About a dozen years ago, the missing piece finally came to light. While I always believed that I had a soul, I scarcely knew anything about it. I'd paid little attention to this aspect of myself, favoring my mind instead. No wonder that I had felt like I was trying to steer a canoe in strong currents—without a paddle.

It was a shock to realize how unacquainted I was with my soul. Getting to know myself in this way would involve my choices, my spiritual life, and the kind of belonging I'd always sought. I could see it would be a lifelong quest. Even if I uncovered only a portion of my soul, what a blessing that would be.

It was time for me to go to work, time to wake up. I didn't have a clue where to start, so I reverted to an old standby: giving myself prompts. Reminders had helped me break through old habits in the past. So I put entries on my work calendar. I wrote sticky notes saying, "Wake Up!" and placed them on my computer monitor and bathroom mirror. It was a simple start.

When I went to bed at night and woke up in the morning, I spoke out loud "I open to my soul" or "Wake up, Molly. It's time to wake up." I didn't only say the words, though—I *felt* them as best I could. I breathed more deeply and steadily. And I allowed my senses to be heightened the way they are when I hike deep into a forest and become keenly aware of my surroundings. (Occasionally my mind protested that I was inventing all of this. I noted my mind's opinion and kept going.)

I'd been a beginner at many things in my life. I knew how awkward and unsure it can be. This beginning of waking up was unique because I actually trusted myself from the start. I was very aware of what I was feeling and thinking. I took actions that suited me, not selfish ones, but those that aligned with what felt true to me.

About a month into my commitment, a different statement came to mind:

"I am awake and fully conscious."

These new words lifted my spirits when I spoke them. I made new sticky notes right away. Finally, I told close friends and family members what I was doing; after all, the yellow stickies in every direction were pretty obvious.

I whispered my new commitment when I drove my car and while working at my desk. Sitting in meetings, I made sure to hear the words "awake" and "conscious" in my mind. At least thirty times a day, *yes, at least thirty,* I spoke out loud, "I am awake and fully conscious."

Using the words "I am" was empowering to me. It affirmed my individual aliveness. It spoke to me that I existed and I mattered and that a more satisfying life was at hand, one marked by joy and peace. The words gave me hope that somehow I might come into my authentic self.

OPEN TO SOUL

Opening to your soul has many benefits. It presents a much bigger playing field than the one formed by the old patterns you've known. You'll become more attuned to what you're doing and saying. The accuracy of your impressions—what you see, hear, and sense—goes up. I'm describing the experience of a deeper and more meaningful reality as you go about your daily activities.

Give some thought to your own interest in waking up spiritually. Is it time for you to take baby steps forward as I did? Remember that you're the agent of your experience in life. Every day you get to *choose* how you're going to approach the rest of it. Maybe you're like the plum sapling I mentioned, and intention and movement can get you started.

Heading in a new direction spiritually can be challenging. There's comfort to be found in the words of the Old Testament's 23rd Psalm. Its verses assure you of several things including:

> You won't be left wanting or lacking.
> Your soul *can* be restored to its rightful place.

~~~~~ **GUIDED PRACTICE** ~~~~~

Beginning to awaken is having new eyes for seeing and new ears for listening. The world around you has an aliveness to it that you didn't notice before. A new awareness may be expanding within you. Craft a brief phrase or sentence to help you focus on waking up. Write it in your journal. Begin to use this waking-up prompt in your daily life.

After three days have gone by, jot down your thoughts about the following:

+ What does it mean to you to be a beginner? When you've been brand-new at an activity, how did you manage? What are the upsides of being a beginner?
+ I've encouraged you to focus your attention on waking up. If you've done this, what subtle changes, if any, have you noticed as you've gone through your day? What's different in your interactions with others?

Some of us like to read an entire book without stopping to do the exercises. That's understandable. If you're in this group, I hope you'll circle back soon. There's tremendous value in journaling for this kind of work.

MY HAPPINESS GROWS
IN DIRECT PROPORTION TO
MY ACCEPTANCE, AND IN
INVERSE PROPORTION
TO MY EXPECTATIONS.

MICHAEL J. FOX

Releasing Expectations

BECOMING AWARE of what hinders our soulful path is part of waking up. A common roadblock is having expectations of how life should be. These preset ideas cloud our perspective. Instead of having inner connectedness, we look outwardly and start to make comparisons. It's a quick route to unhappiness.

From an early age, we develop a set of expectations of life. These are thought forms that arise from our experiences. Activities, decisions, judgments, opinions, beliefs, and mental images all contribute to this storehouse within us. We're influenced, also, by the expectations of others, whether family, friend, boss, or pastor.

Expectations offer some benefits in helping you navigate through life. Uncertainty is reduced, and you may be better prepared for what comes next. Contracts for services are a type of expectation. For example: "I expect my doctor to treat me when I'm sick" or "My mechanic will fix my car."

If you take time to analyze your expectations, you'll discover your underlying beliefs about health, family, home, religion, career, money, and a lot more. Some of them are quite reasonable and ordinary. Think of "My car will start up this morning" and "I'll save money by using Wednesday coupons."

Expectations also have a painful side, and that's what we want to examine. These mental patterns can lead us to try to control the people and events in our lives. When coupled with low self-esteem, expectations are especially detrimental, as in these examples:

If I'm not successful, that means I'm a loser.
Compared to her, I'm not attractive enough.
My dad doesn't spend time with me. I must not be lovable.

Expectations try to dictate what you and others *should* do, think, and believe. What *should* happen now and in the future are in our expectations, along what *should've* happened in the past. When there's a discrepancy between an expectation and the reality that occurs, a whirlpool of emotions is unleashed. It's very uncomfortable, and the voice of your soul gets lost in the tumult.

THE PROBLEM OF EXPECTATIONS

Throughout my childhood and as an adult, I had high expectations. I could've named them *Great Expectations*, but the title was already taken. I anticipated a lot from other people and held the highest requirements for myself. Whether it was supervisors not taking needed action or friends behaving badly, *people didn't act the way I thought they would.*

I was crushed at every disappointment. Thwarted expectations underscored my lack of self-worth. Naively, I assumed that most people would share my values or at least respond in a straightforward way. When some of them acted at cross-purposes to my interests, I felt downgraded. This is how I came to believe that expectations can ruin our chances to be happy.

We need to pay close attention to expectations because they're stealthy, demanding, and persistent mind-sets. They're *stealthy* because they formed outside of our awareness. We had no chance to give a conscious up or down vote on these powerful influences. Expectations are *demanding* because they compel us to think and act in ways that can be less than soulful. Deeply ingrained, their laws rule our behavior. Expectations are also *persistent.* Unless we intervene, they continue to be the lenses through which we view the world.

Expectations are carriers of some of our most entrenched beliefs. And the effects of those beliefs on one's life can be devastating. For example, if I had been deeply hurt as a child and carried the belief that people who loved me would also hurt me, think about the consequences. I'd live life *unconsciously* expecting love and hurt to go together. It seems to me that this is how we can create the very things we fear.

Our objective is to see how our mind and emotions can *support* soulfulness, not block it. For now, it's enough to know that expectations can set you up for a fall. No one warns you that you'll be trying endlessly to reconcile the movie playing in your head with the utter reality of daily living.

〜〜〜 GUIDED PRACTICE 〜〜〜

Think about a recent time in your life when you expected someone to act in a particular way. You thought they *should* behave that way because it made perfect sense—to you! Instead, they chose a different course. Their behavior didn't match your expectations.

In your journal, write down every detail you can remember.

+ What went on inside of you, e.g., your thoughts, feelings, inner dialogue, or replaying of the scene?
+ What underlying beliefs of yours might have contributed to this incident?

EXPECTATION CONSCIOUSNESS

Hanging on to expectations is like having to pull a heavy suitcase down a sidewalk. Bulging and lopsided with beliefs about how life should be, it won't roll properly on its wheels. At the slightest bump, the bag tends to fall over and cause a scene.

In favor of your soul, I'm suggesting that you become vigilant about your expectations. Recognize them when they show up. Decide how you're going to respond. Will you be devastated or at least set back if they're not met?

You picked up expectations along your life's journey, unconsciously. Now it's time to attend to them, *consciously*, like any habit that may not be healthy for you. The idea here is to handle, with grace, the thought patterns you identify. Apply any elements from your own spiritual practices and beliefs to help you in the process.

There's a stark difference between an expectation and an observation. To observe something is to notice its qualities without judging what you think it ought to be. For instance, you can look at an art sculpture in a gallery. See its shape, hues, and materials. You can wonder what the artist might've been thinking regarding the design. You notice if you have a preference for it or not. What you're not doing is telling yourself that you'd never pay $6,000 for that piece of junk.

Similarly, you can decide to go to your favorite restaurant. The wait for a table at 5 p.m. is one-and-a-half hours. You notice the crowd; your special eating spot has become quite popular. You're too hungry to wait that long. You'll miss the food, but it's time to drive elsewhere. What you're not doing is fuming inside about how your personal venue has been stolen from you. Begin to understand how *observations can promote peace of mind*.

Besides paying attention to your thoughts, I'll be encouraging you to use your imagination as a tool for healing. If you've not done this kind of thing before, it might seem strange. Remember when you were a kid and your imagination would go wild? Did it open great vistas and new worlds for you to explore? Mine did. At any age, we can benefit from the freedom of imagination.

While learning a skill, I remind myself that I'm a beginner on a new journey. I say that I'm practicing the new behavior; that way I don't feel like I have to do it perfectly. For the time being, you can practice identifying your expectations.

~~~~ GUIDED PRACTICE ~~~~

WITNESS. One step in claiming a life of soul is learning to recognize expectations. Spend a week paying attention to the expectations you hear around you, as well as your own. Don't judge yourself or have opinions about others, just listen. Notice how folks (and you) respond when their expectations aren't met. IDENTIFY. You've had a week of witnessing expectations. Now, look to see if any upsets you've felt had a source in your expectations. Recall when you were uncomfortable or unhappy in any interactions and finish these sentences in your journal:

I expected _____.
What happened was _____.
There's a discrepancy here that bothers me: _____.

EXPLORE. Exploration means that you examine your options. It helps if you don't have to take immediate action in the situation, especially when it involves another person. Wait until you feel more stable and peaceful. Do you see how self-awareness can interrupt the cycle of upset?

As you explore options, one choice for you is to stop being bothered by the discrepancy. Can you live just fine without taking action in this case? Can you just let it go? When there's not a lot at stake, this can be easy.

Following up on your unmet expectation is another choice. You can take additional actions to increase the chance of getting what you want. Is it a case of needing to express yourself more clearly? Write down specifics about your unmet expectation and, with a calm mind, discuss it with the other people involved.

REDIRECT. Remember how you committed to waking up? Your senses became more alert as you practiced wakefulness. Notice that you're able to do the next exercise because of your heightened awareness.

As soon as you realize an expectation has started to play out, take stock. Say to yourself, "Whoa, there's an expectation here. I'm going to let it pass on through." Watch the expectation as it moves through you and see it leave. Breathe fully and steadily.

We're working on ways to refocus our mental energy. In case you enjoy using your imagination, I'll mention a couple of options for redirecting your attention. One is to form a mental image of the expectation and see it right in front of you. Give the expectation a size, shape, and color, if you'd like, or see it contained within a box. As you observe the object, begin to see it dissipate into thin air. How do you feel now? The original thought pattern may be present still, but the emotional charge could be reduced or gone.

Alternatively, you could envision yourself holding the expectation image or box in your hands. Now, hand it over to your choice of an angel, prophet, or saint who will take it away promptly. As you let it go, state out loud: "I release you (type of expectation) now. I claim only goodness and love."

WAVE OF EXPECTATIONS

My own experience of addressing expectations was different than what I've recommended for you. I didn't have a road map to guide me.

Some years ago, things came to a crescendo in my life. Too many stressors happened at once, creating what psychotherapists have called a "pile-on effect." Door after door had seemingly slammed in my face over several months. Work projects had dried up, money was tight, and two longtime friendships faded. I questioned where and how I was fitting in the world. In the midst of this, my dad injured himself in a fall, and one month later we held his funeral. My older brother gave the eulogy. Three days later, *he* died unexpectedly. Allow me to bring you into that moment:

> *No one else is at home today. I walk into the living room in the late afternoon. Golden light pours through our front windows. I stop between the couch and fireplace as sorrow and disappointment hit me hard. It feels like I might bust open.*
>
> *All of a sudden, I'm terribly uncomfortable and light-headed. Oh, it's my lungs—they're craving oxygen. I forgot to breathe, so I reach for the couch and begin to breathe in as deeply as I can. I sit down and breathe out. I keep taking deep breaths and releasing them. After a couple of minutes, I start to feel better.*
>
> *My mind is trying to make sense of what's happening to me. The recent losses are significant, but they're not all of it. No, it's also the unrealistic expectations I've had of myself—of where I thought I'd "be" at this stage in life. High expectations of others and of myself have run me forever. I can't do it anymore. Words tumble out of my mouth before I know it.*
>
> *"Stop! Stop it, Molly! Just stop!" I shout this—to the world, life in general, and myself in particular. A dove roosting in a juniper next to the house startles and flutters away.*
>
> *Putting a halt to my expectations means that I'll have to stop trying to figure out life to the nth degree. No more habitual thinking-ruminating-analyzing mental loops. I don't know*

how I'm going to do it, but it's going to happen. I can feel my resolve.

Instead of thinking about my situation, I focus on breathing. Breathe in, breathe out. The repetition feels good. My mind stays still, my body relaxed. Hands in my lap, I watch household dust swirl in the sun's last rays. Then I have a thought about having no thoughts, and I almost smile.

It occurs to me that I've finally confronted my expectations. It took this crisis for me to finally say "Enough!" I wonder what life beyond expectations will be like. I have no idea. My husband will think I'm on a new tangent; he's a kind man and will refrain from rolling his eyes.

The room is dark now, so I stand up and turn on a lamp. I'm going to take things moment by moment. This is all new.

Throwing off expectations in the way I did that day was a catharsis for me, a purifying, cleansing release. It shook me out of my old, stubborn patterns.

Several days floated by, "float" being the correct word. I attended to the routines of my work and personal life. Basics got done—like meals, laundry, e-mails, and phone calls. I had a kind of guilty pleasure in keeping my mind from racing ahead.

When I recognized that an expectation was launching in me, I stopped what I was doing and relaxed. I found I could monitor this pretty well. Occasionally, in a quiet and unassuming tone, I'd tell another person about an expectation that I was having.

Something about speaking it out loud allowed me to stay calm.

Without old expectations to guide my behavior, everything had a temporary feel, like traveling solo in a foreign land. I wasn't my former self, the one I knew well. I handled only what was right in front of me. I knew that this adjustment was going to take some time.

SELF-CARE

For some of us, the work has just begun in managing our troublesome expectations. Like most things, it will get easier with practice. Awareness of expectations becomes a part of our lifelong discipline of self-care.

You're bound to lapse into judgments or opinions here and there. But be forgiving of yourself when it happens. Don't build up expectations about letting go of your expectations. When you realize you're having an expectation, say to yourself, "Oh, there's another one. Hmm." Notice how you react to it. See if you can let go of the expectation right then, along with any emotions that have surged along with it.

When we take our power back from the grip of expectations, we become more present, alert, and peaceful. Our soul has more access to us. This is how we're entitled to live. Be gentle and kind to yourself as you explore this new territory. You're on your way, so stay with it, my friend.

CAN YOU REMAIN
UNMOVING TILL THE RIGHT
ACTION ARISES BY ITSELF?

Lao Tzu

Becoming Stillness

EMBRACING MEDITATION

WE'RE ABOUT TO TAKE A RIGHT TURN on our soul's journey. You won't want to miss this. I'll be sharing my unfolding story about learning to be still and how stillness and the soul walk together. Hands down, it's the most important concept in this book.

A few weeks after my crisis of expectations, I began to realize something. It was more of a feeling than a thought. Quietly, yet persistently, the message kept coming to mind:

It is good for me to meditate.

Meditation means being present in the moment while cultivating inner stillness. Only a few decades ago, it was considered a mostly Eastern practice. Now meditation and its proven health benefits are in the mainstream. The activity of meditating calms negative emotions and relaxes the mind and body. It reduces stress and boosts the immune system. Many people use it to manage pain and control symptoms of illness. Mental awareness can also be increased.

I'd known for years about meditation. In the early 1990s, I'd led a contemplative prayer class, which was an introduction to meditative techniques. But after that, I kept coming up with one excuse after another to not meditate. I was too busy. Surely I was a person who really didn't need to meditate—I'd do fine without it. Meditating for me meant getting up earlier, and for a time I wasn't sleeping well. Later I thought I could meditate while walking for exercise. (Multitasking!) The bottom line was that I hadn't made a commitment to it.

From experience, I knew that meditation was a route to inner harmony. Yet my mind continued to resist the idea of sitting still. "It is good for me to meditate" knocked on the door of my heart. I figured the message came from my soul, so I'd better pay attention this time. After all the work that I'd done on waking up and managing my unruly expectations, why not?

> *I decided to practice right away while I felt encouraged. So I set a kitchen timer for thirty minutes, sat in a quiet corner, and commenced. I didn't expect anything to happen in particular, reminding myself that I was a beginner.*
>
> *With my mouth closed, I inhaled a full breath through my nose and held it for three or four seconds. Then I exhaled slowly,*

gently expelling all the air I could from my lungs. I repeated the series of breaths five times and then began to breathe normally. Hey, I'm doing pretty well so far.

Suddenly my mind wandered. Had I entered yesterday's bank deposit in the register twice or just once? I knew enough about meditation to (1) not resist the thoughts that showed up and (2) be accepting of myself. Gently, I brought my mind back to stillness. I focused exclusively on breath in, breath out, breath in, breath out.

Another set of thoughts intruded. I got up and started playing soft instrumental music from my laptop. Nice touch. It seemed that a lot of time went by. Could my timer be broken?

I told myself to remain quiet. Stillness. A Bible verse came to mind: "Be still and know that I am God." (Psalm 46:10) I envisioned those words printed on the inside of my closed eyelids. By learning to be still, I might know something of God. It's a profound promise, this matter of stillness, and it had been easy to ignore.

Finally, the timer beeped to end my first meditation session in years. A pretty decent job for someone just getting underway. My body felt nurtured, my mind calm. Sitting in the chair, I felt a keen sense that all is well. Not just one part of life or another, but all of it. I promised to pay more attention to my inner promptings. Now that my mind was quieter, I could hear them better.

OASIS OF STILLNESS

I invite you to get acquainted with stillness as part of your journey of soul. It can become your best friend. Meditation is a way to tune in to your deepest self as well as the divine realm. Your soul may speak to you in that stillness—certainly that's been my experience. Over time, you'll notice that your mind becomes more calm, focused, and balanced.

Many different forms of meditation exist: silent, guided, focused on an object or word, music, no music, walking, standing, sitting. For this book, I've kept it simple. What's important is for you to choose what suits your personality. Then do your best to get still for a few minutes, every day if you can.

There's a contemplative practice known as mindfulness meditation. It involves using breath as the focus of your awareness. Because of my overactive mind, mindfulness meditation was (and is) the best option for me. I noticed how it felt to breathe in and breathe out to a regular rhythm. As soon as a random thought showed up, I returned to awareness of my breathing. The cycle of stillness, to thought, and back to stillness would happen several times in a session. Each moment of stillness became a precious oasis for me. It fueled the rest of my day with balance and calm.

~~~~~ GUIDED PRACTICE ~~~~~

Meditation is the practice of inner stillness. When you medi-tate regularly, you discover a most magnificent part of yourself. This quiet place within you becomes like a deep pool of water, one you can float in. It's so safe and nurturing that you'll *want* to go there often. Meditation/stillness is not an escape from life, though. Rather, it's a recharge zone where you connect with your authentic self.

If you've not meditated previously, you might wonder how a person gets started. First, give up any preconceived ideas that there's a "right" way to do it. Meditation can be practiced a hun-dred different ways. Simply decide that you're going to explore the stillness within you.

Go to a room where you'll have solitude for at least a half hour. It helps if the room has a peaceful feel and is uncluttered. You can light a candle if that's soothing to you. Sit in a comfort-able chair with good support. Let your body relax and feel at one with this setting. Your eyes may be closed or open.

Take five deep, slow breaths, holding each breath for two or three seconds before slowly exhaling. Resume normal breathing. Tell your mind that it's okay to be calm. Meditation is a time for taking a break from thinking. Focus exclusively on your breath in, breath out. Some folks get frustrated because their minds race around when they try to be still. When a thought intrudes, the moment you realize it, return your focus to your breathing, and the thought will evaporate.

One day a friend shared a technique from her spiritual tradition regarding interfering thoughts. I've enjoyed using it. At the moment you become aware of having a thought, see a soft white feather gently tap on the thought as a reminder to return to your breathing. Inhaling and exhaling, you sit in quiet.

Take an inventory of how your body feels. In your journal, reflect on the meditation you just completed:

- If this was your first time to meditate, did the focus on breathing help to quiet your mind?
- If stillness has been a longtime practice for you, what did you notice today?

BRAIN WAVE PATTERNS

When meditating, we're in a state of lower-frequency brain waves. Brain wave patterns affect everything from how we learn, to how we accomplish tasks, to how readily we go to sleep at night. I'm not a neuroscientist, but I'll share what I've learned and how brain waves have influenced my meditation practice.

Greatly simplified, there are four primary brain wave patterns in adults. (Children's patterns are different.) Experts categorize them by frequency, which is the number of cycles or repetitions observed in a one-second time frame, measured in hertz (Hz).

Beta (13+ Hz) brain waves relate to the active, daytime mind. All five senses are activated, and the eyes are generally open while we're listening, thinking, talking, and solving problems. A stressed-out person's brain waves will be in the upper ranges of Beta, which is not a healthy place over the long term, apparently. In the past, I beta-ed myself up quite a lot.

Alpha (8–12 Hz) is a state of relaxed alertness, good for studying and creativity. *Wish I'd known this in college.* Eyes may be open or closed. Alpha is inspirational and meditative; many of my meditations seem to occur there. Some folks believe that spending time in Alpha can enhance the healing process, which is an excellent thought.

Theta (4–8 Hz) is a deeply meditative, relaxed, and trance-like state. It's where you access subconscious information and memory. Specialists say it can be an effective place for initiating changes in behavior. Theta is associated with intuition, dreaming, and inner guidance. It's also the sweet spot between sleeping and waking—a place for seeing visions and making positive self-suggestions.

Good old Delta (0.5–4 Hz). The body regenerates itself here. In Delta's dreamless sleep, the body becomes completely relaxed. If ever you've been startled while in Delta mode, you know how hard it can be to arouse.

Looking back, I realized that I had spent a lot of my life analyzing, comparing, calculating, and building scenarios. It was over-the-top Beta. It struck me that life wasn't meant to be spent that way. Cultivating lower-frequency brain wave cycles could be healthier and more balanced for me.

I began to practice altering my brain wave pattern to achieve a particular purpose, such as to relax or be more creative. Here's one way I did it. In a quiet, uninterrupted place, I set my desire to enter either the Alpha or Theta state. Then I meditated in the regular way. Occasionally, I would envision myself going down a staircase, starting with an upper landing of Beta and ending at the lower Alpha or Theta floor. When thoughts intruded, I returned gently to awareness of my breathing. (Note that I never did any of this while operating a vehicle or machinery, nor should you.)

Another way I practiced lowering my brain wave frequency was through repetitive, uncomplicated tasks. One day I experienced a positive mental shift while painting a bedroom. After taping the baseboards, I applied paint to the walls methodically using a roller and paintbrushes. My mind was in a meditative state of concentration without any noticeable effort. There's something about physical repetition that can put a person into the Alpha state. I've also had it happen to me while exercising.

I don't own an EEG (electroencephalograph) to properly measure my brain waves. Instead, I assessed that I'd reached

Alpha or Theta by how my body felt and the way my mind responded. In Alpha, I felt calm and yet alert at the same time. That's why it's an especially sweet place for learning new subjects.

In Theta, especially at the lower-frequency brain waves within that range, I've found myself in deep meditative trances. I no longer felt my body's weight against the chair or heard outside noises. It can be a beautiful place to go. To experience the feeling that your soul abides within you, seek Theta. You'll understand what I mean.

Spending time in Theta gives you access to a deep part of yourself. One day I utilized Theta brain waves to help me make a key decision:

A job offer I received had many pluses and a few potential minuses. After going meditatively into (what I believed to be) Theta with my question, an image appeared. It was a set of French doors located on the side of a large brick home. The glass panels were fogged over and, as an entrance, it looked unused. When I tried the knob, it wouldn't budge. I remember thinking "I can't go in." Right then I became more alert, perhaps in upper Alpha or lower Beta, and I opened my eyes.

I felt grateful to have received such a clear answer. It was like finding the one puzzle piece that brings the rest of the picture together. Because of what I saw, I knew I would not take that job.

〜〜〜 GUIDED PRACTICE 〜〜〜

Note: Persons with medical conditions involving the brain should not work with brain wave patterns before seeking professional advice.

If you have a bit of information you want to learn, or you'd like to memorize a short poem, begin to meditate in your regular way. After about ten minutes, pick up the text and speak the words out loud at a leisurely pace. Use as many of your senses as you can while you read. Pause for a minute; then repeat the process three more times. Do this for several days. Assess how well you're remembering the material. What have you discovered about learning while in the Alpha brain wave state? Make notes in your journal.

Begin the practice of making a positive statement to yourself as you're drifting off sleep at night and as you begin to awaken in the morning. These are times when you're likely in the Theta brain wave pattern. Here's an example of a positive self-statement: "I am profoundly grateful for this day." Craft a simple statement that speaks to you. Use the same statement for three weeks. After that time, see what you have noticed, if anything. In your journal, write about your experience.

CREATIVE MEDITATION

Your practice of meditation may change over time. It could be because you're following your heart. I experimented with standing meditation for a while before shifting to a mindfulness approach. In my case, focusing on my breath helped me manage any intruding thoughts.

Many meditation teachers encourage their students to envision a sacred space in their minds. It becomes a nurturing place to go during a session, such as a garden, cottage, or mountain glen. In your case, choose whatever helps you relax and enjoy the meditation experience.

One thing I know about myself is that I'm a very visual person. I like to see and interact with images and color. (You may be this way too, or you might respond more to readily sound and music or movement.) Because I'm so visual, I created in my mind a scene set in the northern part of the U.S. West Coast, or maybe I should say that it chose me. I use it often when I meditate.

The sacred space I visit is a small beach, rocky in spots, with dark-green-forested hills behind it. The air is cool, but I never need a jacket. Fish jump beyond the sandbar. I hear a foghorn in the distance and smell the salt water. Terns scurry ahead as I walk barefooted on white sand. The sun peeks over the horizon. Occasionally, I hear a pod of whales blowing in the deeper water. Sounds idyllic, doesn't it? That's okay because the scene is mine—it can be as perfect as I desire it to be. You can do the same for yourself.

I've had surprises while meditating on "my" beach. One day when I was deep in meditation, I heard thrashing noises from the tree line. I turned around as a sizable black bear emerged from the woods. She lumbered toward me. Somehow I knew it was a she-bear, and I stood rock still, feeling vulnerable and anxious. The bear stopped right next to me and looked out over the water. After a minute, I placed my arm gingerly across her back. I felt the coarseness of her hair, the warmth of her skin, how her body expanded with each noisy breath. Unlike a dog, the bear wasn't overly friendly to me, but she was attentive in a detached way. I could tell she was a force for good and should be respected.

The bear joined me on the beach several other times; once she brought along a playful cub. There was nothing overtly communicated between the three of us. It was a shared presence more than anything.

I didn't expect a bear to show up in my meditations. Many native cultures view them as a powerful totem. In my case, the bear's strength and grounding energy were amazing. Coincidentally, "Bear" was a nickname of mine growing up; family members and a couple of close friends still use it.

On most days, my meditations were (and are) pleasant and routine experiences. Occasionally, my body and mind relax so much that I become semiconscious. I like it when I go that deep.

I'll see different scenes and people's faces. It's similar to dreaming in that way. Often I don't have a clue what the images mean.

Meditation is the starting point for huge personal change. Ask yourself if you're ready to commit to daily meditation. If so, say yes by making room for it in your life now.

You can work through any mental roadblocks or feelings of incompetence. Practicing meditation on a daily basis will be enormously helpful. Books and DVDs are available to guide you with techniques. Community classes offer a group experience. Phone apps are also available for meditation and brain wave practice. There's a way that will work best for you, so find it.

⌒ Milestone ⌒

It's been said that every ending marks a new beginning. We've completed three chapters, so it's time to check on our progress.

In working together, we've committed to waking up spiritually. We've become aware of our expectations and have options for handling them. Our minds are more peaceful because we're not drawn into so many unconscious upsets. Finally, we've begun to know the gifts of stillness.

There's been a shift from an outward focus to greater attention toward your inner life. Take time to acknowledge your courage and commitment. Answer the following questions in your journal:

- What have you observed about your deepening spirituality and wakefulness?
- How have you managed your expectations?
- What do you experience while being in stillness?
- What's new or fresh about you, however subtle?
- What are you curious about now?

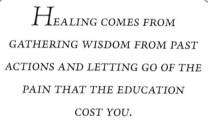

Healing comes from gathering wisdom from past actions and letting go of the pain that the education cost you.

Caroline Myss

Looking Back and Moving Forward

NEXT TO THE FRONT DOOR of our home in Texas is a chunk of rock with an embedded rope handle. Less than a foot in diameter and four inches tall, it doesn't look like much. For me, though, it's a connection to history, family, and a much older house that once stood eighty miles north of here. My great-grandfather built it in 1898 to accommodate his wife and fourteen children.

These ancestors settled in an area that is notorious for tornadoes. It's not surprising that they anchored the home's wood framing every few feet using a footing of concrete, limestone rocks, and rope. The ranch house lasted at least until 1939, when the U.S. government claimed the entire region to construct Fort Hood.

In 1994 a dozen family members and I sought out the old homestead. With the commander's permission and aerial maps, we scoured what had become a tank practice area. Hours later, chilled and soggy from persistent drizzle, we got out of the vehicles and literally stumbled across part of the homestead's foundation. The old footings were broken to pieces and scattered on the hilltop. Looking more closely, we found several of them intact, treasures all, and one came home with me.

It was quite a process to seek out the old place, stand on its ground, and leave with a tangible piece of my family's history. Our brief time on that hill was filled with reverence. Even now, I come in the front door and look down at the stone in acknowledgment. I think of what makes up the foundation of my own life. Do those qualities support a life of soul?

This chapter is about taking time to look back at life from a distance. We'll stay in the past only as long as necessary. There will be time to make sense of it, glean wisdom, and/or let it go. Our journey points always in the direction of wholeness.

Readiness and courage are important companions as we revisit the past. Some memories carry negative emotions and self-defeating beliefs. Our desire for healing supports us in the process. It may seem overwhelming or frightening to delve into the past; a professional therapist can help.

Dealing with unfinished business in life can be liberating. I know this firsthand. Unhealthy scenarios no longer suck me in as they once did. I don't have to bury my feelings, protect secrets, or keep up my defenses, which I did for so many years.

LIFE REVIEWS

The process we'll be following is called a life review. It's a written inquiry that allows you to revisit the events and people of your past in a deliberate way. You'll record key points that have shaped your life. Afterwards, you can examine them on your own or discuss them with another person.

Different forms of life reviews have been used by social workers and counselors for many years, formally and informally. Oftentimes, elderly and terminally ill individuals go through a life review process to help bring them closure and as an overall sense making activity.

In some spiritual traditions, life reviews are thought to be led by angelic beings after one's death. Scenes from a person's earthly life play like an animated slide show, revealing the good and bad, hurt and joy, love and disappointment. Movies such as *Defending Your Life* have dramatized these afterlife life reviews.

I've heard survivors of near-death experiences mention having a life review while out of the body. While they felt accountable for their actions on earth, many also reported feeling enveloped by forgiveness and universal love.

Doing a life review can be helpful at any stage of life. We'll approach it as a type of meditation, which you're familiar with now. Remarkable insights are likely to emerge; I know they did for me.

DIFFICULT MEMORIES

Everything that has happened to you has taught you something or allowed you to experience a particular setting or feeling. Look inside of yourself. Do you feel internally strong about moving forward?

I'll share a criticism about life reviews. Some folks believe that it's unnecessary or risky to delve into the past. The concern is that more emotional damage could occur from revisiting instances of trauma, abuse, and violence. If this is your situation, do seek the advice of a trained professional before undertaking a life review. The decision you make will be a soulful response to your individual needs.

I had my share of remembering difficult episodes from my past. Some of them contained extreme emotions such as terror and anger. When feelings other than peace arose, I would pause and diffuse them with love. You'll see what I mean in the incident that follows.

> As a kid, I was having fun swimming in a local public pool with my younger brother and sister. A twelve-year-old relative was also part of our group. At one point, I dove down and swam a few feet underwater. That's when the older boy began to playfully block my coming to the surface. I tried to swim around him but couldn't. When I ran out of oxygen, I panicked. Still, I couldn't get to the surface. I began to sink down in darkness,

no longer struggling. After a short while, I felt an intense pain in my upper arm. With an Ironman grip, the lifeguard was pulling me out.

An event such as this is bound to have emotional fallout. I'd never processed my feelings about it. During my life review, I spoke directly to the memory and my deepest self, saying "Love is all there is." I let the spirit of love infuse the situation as I replayed the scene in my mind. Also, I told the memory that its time had passed: "I live now, in this moment, not then." These are ways that I was able to detach from any charged-up feelings and stay centered.

HOW I BEGAN MY LIFE REVIEW

When I was ready to review my life, I figured that I'd start with childhood. It shocked me to realize what I'd forgotten. For instance, I didn't remember being nine years old. Memories of most birthdays and holidays were just ... not ... there. I recalled grade school teachers and a few close friends, our family home and cherished pets. Clearly this wasn't the best place to launch.

Recent spans of time seemed more manageable for me. So I began by looking at the last ten years, followed by the decade before that. I sat in quietness and asked myself for questions and memories related to that time. As they came to mind, I

thought. Make note of any recurring themes or scenarios, or emotions that were triggered often. Get a sense of the role these emotions played in your life.

Events will be recalled from your own perspective. At times, it might be fruitful to take another point of view. This is optional, of course, but you could explore what it must've been like through your father's or mother's eyes or perhaps a sibling's.

Meantime, here are more questions to consider:

Who were the folks who raised me? Who were the others who grew up with me or around me?

What attributes of my grandparents or other relatives affected our family? What behavioral patterns transferred from them to my immediate family? How did ancestral ties play out in my life?

What influenced me during my most formative years?

What did I lose or miss out on?

What am I grateful for?

What personal gifts did I discover early on?

Throughout the life review process, be kind and nurturing to yourself. If it becomes overly painful, set the work aside. This creates a safe distance between you and any unhealed parts of you. You can return to the life review later or not at all. I've mentioned therapy as a safe place to deal with a painful past. Your job is to take care of *you* first.

DOWN BELOW AND UP ABOVE

Earlier I told the story of the foundation stone that sits on our front porch. You know that a foundation is the backbone of a house. It supports the way the whole structure fits together. No amount of window dressing on the top side of a house can correct a foundation problem.

Every life has its foundational elements also. Your own foundations will show up consistently in your life review. Take a look at the strong underpinnings that have guided how you've lived. Perhaps you see qualities of strength and resilience or a hearty sense of humor.

It's possible that a weakened part of your internal foundation may have come to light. In my life review, I saw underpinnings of fear and insecurity, which don't make for a stable foundation. This wasn't the first time it had come up either. A wise friend had pointed it out when I was in my mid-thirties. I'll take you back to that time.

Grace and I had met late in her life. There was a fifty-year difference in our ages. This plainspoken retired school nurse and devout Episcopalian was like a beloved aunt to me. As our friendship grew, she'd heard me tell about the bouts of anxiety I'd had as a child. How my mom checked me out of grade school for occasional long weekends away so that I could rest and regain my equilibrium. Our family doctor said I was sensitive and high-strung. By adolescence, those feelings had gone below the surface. Outwardly, I'd learned to put on a good face.

Feeling deep-down insecurity was a normal state for me—unconscious, habitual, and familiar. I imagine much of it came as a result of my being victimized by a family acquaintance when I was quite young. Somewhere in those years, I had decided that life wasn't to be trusted.

I've lived long enough now to know the high price of having foundational fear. It's an insidious condition which blocks inner peace and keeps company with sadness and depression. All of these conditions hinder the soul.

One day Grace and I were talking over a bowl of soup when she said:

> *"Honey, you never developed a security about life. I can see that."*
> *"What do you mean?" I asked.*
> *"Well, there are lucky folks like me who got all the love and support in the world growing up. I never felt unloved for one moment. You didn't get that sense of safety and protection."*
> *"I never thought of it that way." I put my spoon down, stunned. She was right.*
> *"You missed a foundation that caused you to feel anxious much of the time." Certainly, that part was true.*
> *My voice low and unsure, I asked, "What do I do about it?"*
> *The best I can remember from so many years ago, her answer was "Ask God to heal the hole in you."*

Until Grace spoke, I hadn't connected the way I'd felt inside to the circumstances of my childhood. Then a couple of weeks after our lunch, I attended a lecture by the nationally known rabbi and psychotherapist, Edwin Friedman. His topic for the day was leadership, but a single sentence on the screen is what grabbed me:

Anxiety in the system must be reduced in order to broaden possible responses.

I scribbled down the quote and read it over and over, letting the words sink in. Dr. Friedman was a systems theorist, a specialist in family dynamics. Trained in looking at the situational whole, he knew about the limiting factor of fear—how it causes you to live with blinders on, and you don't even know it. A light bulb switched on for me. I saw how important it was going to be to heal the hole in me.

I knew I needed a systematic approach for such a deep-seated foundation, so I found a professional therapist. Counseling provided enough of an emotional boost to keep me going. I continued to do my own personal work by asking myself questions and responding in my journal. In quiet moments, I'd occasionally look inward at where the gaping hole in me resided. I was encouraged because it seemed to be shrinking.

~~~~ GUIDED PRACTICE ~~~~

Look at the life review notes in your journal. These pages hold clues to your consistent behaviors and responses to situations. It's time to identify your core values—the foundations that have directed how you've shown up in life. Consider answering the following questions in your journal:

- In looking at the cornerstones of your life, which of your foundations have been positive ones?
- Which other foundations, if any, have seemed to block your personal growth or satisfaction?
- Which foundations surprised you or confirmed what you already knew?
- What emotions, if any, are tied to your foundations?

REPAIRING FOUNDATIONS

An inner sense of safety and security was something I'd longed to have. Nearing age fifty and already a grandmother, I couldn't remember ever feeling truly at ease. My life review was mostly done. I felt ready to claim what I'd obviously missed out on.

Having no clue of how a change in me would happen, I kept it simple. I wrote a statement that reflected my deepest intention for safety and protection. Intentions are agreements that you make with yourself. They're like contracts. Intentions represent what you stand for in life and help you focus on desired outcomes. We've used them already in this book.

By declaring a foundation of safety and security for myself, I was making a new choice. The act of consciously choosing is empowering in itself. Within my choice was the belief that *God has my back.* I wasn't alone and didn't need to remain on guard toward life. Finally, I was in a position to accept this.

After some editorial tweaking, here was my declaration:

I'm safe and protected in all places and at all times.

I confirmed my safety and protection by stating it out loud at least five to ten times a day. I knew that intentions are strengthened by imagery, so I envisioned my body infused with safety and security. Closing my eyes, I saw myself walking around feeling confident.

How could I access those feelings when they were so foreign to me? This is the beautiful part of working with intentions and making declarations. Often we'll receive just what we need to make them happen. In my case, a memory came back to me of a time ten years earlier when I'd felt completely safe.

I'd been invited to present a communication workshop to a group of Texas Rangers, a storied and elite group of law enforcement officers. In a meeting room in Austin, surrounded by eleven armed rangers, I felt safe to the very core of my being. Together we did some great work that day.

During our session, my inner guardedness dropped away, and my body relaxed. Joy swelled up in me. These changes were so pronounced that I had to concentrate to stay in charge of the workshop. I remember thinking how great it would be to feel that way always.

I continued to declare my safety and security every day for several months, calling on my feelings from the ranger workshop as needed. One morning during meditation, I received what I'd call a foundational boost. It's an example of the divine support we receive in making positive life changes.

I was focusing on my breath when suddenly I found myself on the sacred beach I mentioned earlier. (Just so you know, when I have a vision, I can see myself in the scene and participate "bodily" at the same time.)

Walking along the shoreline, I began to levitate, floating about five feet above the sand. (If you've ever experienced flying in a dream, you know how freeing and natural it feels.) Other people arrived at the scene, and they were also floating above the ground. We appeared to be waiting for something to happen.

After a while, everyone ascended high above the earth. We flew across vast distances before coming to an unfamiliar landscape. It was covered with hundreds of huge, rusty-red rocks, like in the images you may have seen of Mars's surface.

Each person from the group was guided to land on an individual rock. I sat down on mine and could see other folks doing the same at a distance. It was clear to me that this red land was a place of restoration. I remained there safely and securely for a very long time. Part of me may be there still.

～～～ GUIDED PRACTICE ～～～

You've made a commitment to waking up. Expectations of life are no longer running you the way they once were. Stillness is an important practice. And you've revisited your history. If you've identified any cracks in your life's foundations, this can be a turning point. There are dozens of ways you can adopt a new foundation. Tools from your own spiritual tradition may be valuable in this regard. We'll practice several different options.

Let's say you'd like to develop self-love as one of the cornerstones of your life. You haven't loved or appreciated yourself like you could have. Take your desire for self-love with you into several meditation sessions. Notice what thoughts and images appear to you. What could they mean?

Other action steps can reinforce a foundation of self-love:

+ Create an intentional statement for the new foundation you seek. If you look back at mine, notice that it should contain positive wording and be in the present tense. Find multiple ways to say and use your intention in daily life.

- Write short notes to yourself affirming how lovable you are. (I know, this can seem foolish, but do it anyway. Then order yourself some flowers!)

- Mirror work can be useful. Gaze into your eyes for several minutes, three times a day. While you connect with yourself this way, say: "I love you deeply and completely." (Lock yourself in so you don't get teased by people in your household.)

- Remind yourself often of how lovable you are and express this with gratitude. If there's someone you wished you'd received love from, envision them speaking those words to you.

- Sit on a couch and wrap your arms around your upper body while saying, "I feel great about myself."

- In your journal, write down all of the recent choices you've made in support of self-love, noticing the ways you've acted kindly toward yourself lately.

In case you need a reminder, please be aware that we're divinely supported in our foundational quests, you and I. Continue to give attention to the qualities you seek. Over time, you'll observe that the new foundation has begun integrating within you. Congratulations.

ACCEPTING YOUR WHOLE, ENTIRE LIFE

After reviewing your life's foundations, I hope you've begun to forge stronger ones *by choice*. Hooray for your determination! There's another step to be considered as part of your life review. I recommend it to you wholeheartedly:

Accept the circumstances of your entire life.

To accept your entire life is to receive the whole of it with deep appreciation. You acknowledge what is now and what has been in your world. This is done by you freely and openly, without reservation or judgment, for your spiritual growth. Acceptance is a choice, and it's a beautiful act of love.

The good things that have happened to us are easy to accept. We were lifted up by the positive events and helpful people in our life. Profound losses, traumatic events, acts of violence, and deep disappointments are another matter. If we're shocked and scarred, it can be hard for us to get beyond the pain.

We risk remaining fragmented when we reject portions of our human experience. It's inconsistent with our goal of wholeness. Accepting our life fully brings everything under the soul's care. No longer are we at odds with this or that troubling event or relationship. The pain of being betrayed or mistreated can be released. Energy is freed up for loving ourselves and others.

My invitation is simple: Accept the entirety of what has occurred in your life. There's a kicker here, though—you have to let go of all blame and resentment. Assigning fault to the people, events, and natural disasters is over. Beliefs that "my life is this way because of so-and-so" are based in blame and judgment. It's not necessary to remain a victim, unless that's how you want to view yourself.

One woman I knew well looked back on her life with great regret. Into her eighties, she attributed most of her problems to her mother, who hadn't allowed her to marry the man she loved. Blocked from happiness six decades earlier, she had unwittingly chosen blame as a foundation for the rest of her life.

There's another aspect of giving up blame. You also let go of blaming yourself for what you should've done and didn't. Many of your decisions were based on incomplete information and old behavior patterns. You did the best you could at the time—even if it doesn't seem like it now.

Our mind may put up a roadblock, saying: "Okay, I'll be responsible for my own actions. But why should I accept another person's bad behavior?" This is a valid question. Acceptance doesn't mean that you condone harmful acts. Instead, you are letting go of an unwinnable dispute with reality.

I mentioned that acceptance includes appreciation. How do you have gratitude for the lousy things that occurred? Here's how you do it. You appreciate the difficulty of your situation. The emotions that were triggered. What you gave up. People whom you lost. And how you struggled. Looking through the eyes of love, you're thankful for your strength and resilience. You affirm your love for yourself.

While we don't appreciate harmful acts themselves, we acknowledge how we survived them. Perhaps we're battered and worn, but our soul shines bright. We'll never know why certain things happened. Yet we bring all of our experiences into the soul's fold. Acceptance with appreciation lights our way to inner peace.

Acceptance doesn't happen in an instant, just like your life didn't happen that way. Plan to work with it over time using your life review notes. For some of us, getting to acceptance may be a lifelong quest.

～～～ GUIDED PRACTICE ～～～

Practicing acceptance can be done in a multitude of forms. It's lovely if you feel ready to work with the entirety of your life. But if that's too much too soon, or it's hard to get started, go to your life review pages and select an incident to work with.

Tell yourself that for the next fifteen minutes you're going to fully accept this incident. It can be done as part of your daily meditation or during the Theta brain wave state before sleep.

Use my words or write your own script as you say out loud:

> *I fully accept what has happened to me.*
> *Acceptance brings me peace and wholeness.*
> *I'm grateful for my (entire) life today.*
> *I feel free.*

As you sit in the spirit of acceptance, feel appreciation for the wholeness of your experience. Other emotions may come up, such as compassion and love. Be aware of what this past event has done for you. Perhaps you're seeing your own resilience or feeling empathy for others in similar circumstances. You honor the role this event has played in shaping the person you are.

In your journal, consider the following:

+ What did you experience when practicing acceptance in this brief time frame?
+ What might happen if you accepted your whole, entire life with appreciation?

ENGAGING YOUR BODY

Acceptance with gratitude for your whole, entire life also includes your physical body. It has suffered grief and trauma right along with your mind and heart. This is a substantial topic which is beyond the scope of this book. As you work with your life review, be aware that emotional pain isn't exclusively a brain memory.

When we are hurt by something, the effects may be felt in various parts of our body. For me, that's often been in the abdominal area and occasionally the throat. I first noticed this about twenty years ago during a massage with a new therapist.

Ten minutes into the session, I began to cry. I was embarrassed because nothing had been said or done to launch the tears. The therapist reassured me that sudden tears happened to clients regularly enough. He explained that one of my muscle groups had likely released some stored-up pain during the session.

Another instance of the emotional-physical connection happened soon after my dad died. I began to have intense shoulder pain and couldn't lift my right arm above shoulder level. I wondered if I'd somehow injured my rotator cuff. Before I could get to a medical doctor, I saw an experienced acupuncturist and massage therapist. As he worked on me, he mentioned the number of clients he'd had with shoulder problems, and every one of them had experienced recent grief. Knowing about that connection helped me as I healed.

When a part of my body is compromised and doesn't require immediate medical care, I'll close my eyes and visualize the area during meditation. If it's a sore muscle or an upset stomach, the area might show up in my mind's eye as dense and foggy, perhaps dark in color. I start by thanking my body overall for what it's done for me. (By the way, this is a good daily practice.)

I ask the unwell part of me what it needs. Sometimes there's no reply. Other times I get a sense that love, attention, or rest would help, which I'm willing to give. Through my mind's eye again, I visualize any denseness dispersing into a nearby hole in the earth. I finish by applying a soothing color to the area. When more than this seems to be needed, I'll seek health care advice.

You've learned to calm your mind and use your imagination. During your life review, you asked many types of questions. You can make some similar inquiries of your physical self as a form of meditation.

Sit in a favorite chair and ask to become aware of any places in your body that feel constricted. Your task is to simply notice what comes up. With eyes closed, you can scan parts of your body starting with your feet. Take plenty of time for this exercise, at least twenty minutes. Thank your body for what it shows you. Write about this experience in your journal. Later on you can decide if you want to ask more specific physical questions or pursue healing alternatives.

Taking responsibility for your life through grateful acceptance can help you feel stronger and more alert. It validates the fullness of your experiences in life—the good, the challenging, and the in-between. All are integrated into the you that is emerging. I hope you can begin to see wholeness in your picture.

You may find that you feel unbound. Lighter. Time will tell what it means for you as an individual. In my case, freedom became one of my life's foundations. Considering how insecure I'd been growing up, feeling free on the inside has been indescribably wonderful.

A COMPLETION RITUAL

On the evening I finished my life review, I decided to do an honoring ritual. At first, I held my dog-eared journal with its hodgepodge of paper scraps against my chest. I felt the vitality, depth, and insight it represented. This one small book contained what I remembered about being alive, how I responded to circumstances, and the subtle and not-so-gentle ways my life had been shaped.

I placed my life review journal on the footstool in front of me. I thought to send the spirit of love through its pages. As I held my hands above it, I felt the energy of love flow through my journal for a long time. I prayed for any remaining not-whole (not-holy) parts of me to come together. In the silence that followed, there was a sense of completion. I placed my journal in a desk drawer and went to join my husband in the living room.

Something had shifted inside me, although I couldn't define it right away. A couple of weeks later, I noticed that I'd been feeling better overall. Many loose ends in my life had been righted through the process of acknowledgment, acceptance, gratitude, and release. My soul knew this, and of course it soared!

~~~~ **GUIDED PRACTICE** ~~~~

As a final life review exercise, hold your journal close and ask yourself what type of ritual would help you acknowledge this major accomplishment. Follow through in ways that celebrate the reconciliation you feel inside. Notice the degree to which you can trust life now.

CHOOSE FOR YOURSELVES
THIS DAY WHOM YOU
WILL SERVE.

Joshua 24:15

Whom Do You Serve?

WE'VE BUILT MOMENTUM together toward a soul-sustaining life. Take a moment to consider all the things you've come to terms with and how your awareness has been expanding. Your deepest self has likely come forward in a variety of ways. Can you feel the difference? There's one more piece to look at now: how to use your mind as a trusted ally for the rest of your journey.

In 1979 Bob Dylan recorded a song called "Gotta Serve Somebody." He sang that no matter who we are or what our station in life, we're going to serve someone. In other words, it's in the natural order to serve some*one* or some*thing*. When I listened to the lyrics several years ago, I wondered what part of me was doing the choosing.

The traditional view of service has meant to reach out in support of someone or something. When we serve, we work for or apply our talents to a situation. The qualities of passion and commitment come to mind, especially for parents responsible for raising youngsters, adult children who help their aging parents, men and women who serve the military, and activists pursuing their causes.

Our life review and foundations work have revealed the ways we've served in the past. For many people, career has been a primary focus of service. Some of us have also worked as devoted volunteers for special interests. Others have served in less organized but still meaningful ways. Assuming Bob Dylan is right, and I think he is, let's look underneath our serving to see who's been calling the shots.

Our definition of serving needs to be enlarged because jobs and good deeds are only part of it. In a bigger context, *we serve what we put our attention on*. In your own life, what has consumed a large part of your mental focus and energy? Could this be the thing you've served?

When I probed my own serving, I uncovered a few surprises. The idealist in me wanted to claim higher purposes for my service, such as when I'd been a volunteer leader at a local nonprofit. In truth, what I'd done was to *serve myself*.

To clarify, let's look at the topic of humans and self-interest for a moment. Self-interest is a concern with one's personal agenda. Sometimes self-interest can veer into self-absorption. Social scientists and economists acknowledge in varying degrees that self-interest is what drives our behavior. I looked around at the people I've known and, God bless 'em, I saw a *lot* of self-interest going on.

The next question I asked made me squirm. *Am I self-focused in the same way?* I had to say yes. I'd been as conditioned to it as everyone else.

On somewhat shaky ground at this point, I ventured ahead. *Well, okay then. I'm a complex human being. If I've served myself, what part of "me" did I serve?* The answer came as a revelation: What I'd served were the dictates of my anxiety-fueled mind. Thoughts and related emotions had driven most of my behavior. Where my mind went, I was sure to follow.

What's the problem with this, really? It's that we're on a journey to discover our soul and to *live from that place*. By following my mind's insistent marching orders, my soul as a helpmate had been cut off. I had little access to its limitless wisdom. It didn't occur to me often to seek divine help, visit my heart, or find clarity. My intuition had frequently been ignored in important decision-making. Remember how I described being excessively caught up in Beta mind? I knew that I had to get real and find some kind of personal balance.

~~~~~ **GUIDED PRACTICE** ~~~~~

Consider reflecting on who or what you've served in your daily life. Write about the following in your journal:

+ Who and/or what have you focused much of your attention on?

+ What ways did you serve the people and things you've identified?
+ What inner needs (self-interests) did you fulfill with your service, such as belonging, getting attention, or proving yourself?
+ You've pursued many types of activities in your life. Which ones fed your quest for personal growth, and which ones now look like diversions?
+ Based on what you're uncovering in this exercise, would you like to change your focus? If so, how?

GET ACQUAINTED WITH EGO-MIND

The intuitive mind is a sacred gift and the rational mind is a faithful servant. We have created a society that honors the servant and has forgotten the gift.
Albert Einstein

There's a term that I'll be using as a layperson to describe how the mind influences us and can be influenced: ego-mind. Be aware that psychiatry has its own definitions of ego and mind, which I'm not trained to elaborate on.

Ego-mind isn't the same as our physical brain, which we know to be the primary organ of our central nervous system.

Also, we don't want to get tripped up on the word "ego." Folks who are excessively proud of themselves are said to have big egos. Self-aggrandizing behavior is only one aspect of the ego-mind I'll be referring to.

Simply put, *ego-mind is the everyday mind that you use to interact with the world and to process information.* This mind develops over your lifetime based on genetic predispositions, personality, emotions, knowledge, habits, and skills. An unfathomable number of internal and external factors have impacted your ego-mind. It's a rather broad comparison, but ego-mind functions like a huge software program that's run by coding unique to you alone.

Self-protection is a primary concern of the ego-mind. It brings threats to our awareness and advises us when to fight or flee. Steeped in fear and protectionism, ego-mind is capable of making up things that didn't happen. This is how people who witness the same event may remember it differently.

Coordinating higher brain operations is another major role of the ego-mind. It relates unfamiliar concepts to what is previously known in order to enhance learning. A great deal of knowledge is stored and managed in our ego-minds. Patterns of behavior are also maintained there. They enable us to ride a bicycle, drive a car, dance the tango, swing a golf club, and operate a bulldozer.

What a tremendous asset we have in our ego-mind! It's perfectly natural and an important part of our identity. However, the kicker for our work together is this: *Ego-mind masquerades as our consciousness*. It's only one part of us, yet it parades as the whole enchilada. Believing that ego-mind is our true self is the source of many problems.

LIMITS TO EGO-MIND

The ego-mind is limited in what it can access on its own. That's why it is considered a *localized* intellect. Ego-mind collects data from outside of itself which it weighs, sorts, and assigns probabilities to. Ego-mind's analysis and output isn't as absolute as one might think. Perhaps you can see this in the next example.

Let's say you want to choose a preschool for your child. It's an important decision for you. You can research possibilities online, visit facilities, and speak with faculty and parents. Ego-mind will consider all of these factors and may have a clear front-runner.

Ego-mind can't really determine the best fit for your child because it isn't attuned to other valid ways of knowing, such as feeling, sensing, and intuiting. Reading another person's character—assessing their maturity and determining trustworthiness and integrity—are not ego-mind functions. The ego-mind can offer only an educated guess based on the data collected. For minor decision-making, this might be good enough for you.

There are other problems with how the ego-mind works. Like a stage manager for your life (or in my case, a dictator), ego-mind *wants* to control and organize. It wants to be in full charge. Most of all, it wants to feel safe. Ego-mind worries over our future, so it runs multiple possibilities and calculates their odds. When something does happen to us, the ego-mind looks to our past for what it may mean. This is how we can jump to sudden conclusions.

Ego-mind has a quick trigger for negative emotions. It's reactive and can be quite irrational. If a current incident reminds your ego-mind of a painful memory, feelings accompanying the memory may rise to the surface. In a snap, you're no longer present to the new situation. And your peace of mind? Gone.

I began to train myself to recognize times when my ego-mind was activated and taking the lead. One indicator was when I felt *resistance* to something or someone. Resistance meant that I didn't approve of what was happening, or I didn't like the outcome. One day I obsessed over having to go into a bank branch to resolve a debit card problem. The amount of time I fussed over having to do something about this was much longer than the actual appointment.

There's another way to pinpoint the ego-mind at work. It happens when you have an attack of expectations. You know about this from our earlier work. "I *should* do this," "He *should* do that," or "Things *should* happen this way." The ego-mind has a need to be right. Other people *should* accept its definitions of right and wrong. When stymied, ego-mind has a habit of taking things personally.

I mentioned before that I've expected a lot of myself and others. One afternoon I grabbed a notepad and begin to record these instances:

When I had negative thoughts and feelings

When I felt resistance to something that was happening

When I heard the word *should* in my head

My first entry mentioned a ridiculously long line at the grocery checkout counter. The next one had to do with sloppy weather. Then the number of bills to pay. A canceled lunch date. Going to the dentist. How we should paint the house because it really needs it. The list went on and on, filled with my ego-mind's opinions. The negative mental chatter was *right there* in black and white. It was time to do something.

~~~~ GUIDED PRACTICE ~~~~

Think back over the week and pinpoint a time when your ego-mind became overstimulated. Write in your journal about what happened and how you responded.

+ How did you become aware that your ego-mind was activated?

+ What's different in your awareness now?

EGO-MIND GETS A NEW NAME

Ego-mind had been a familiar but invisible force within me. I saw the free rein it had continually exercised. Many of my choices had been driven by ego-mind's fear and protectionism. When it came down to it, whom had I served? My ego-mind. I was disturbed at having lived my whole life *unaware* of its extreme influence.

It would've been fruitless to try to get my ego-mind to change, so I didn't waste time on that. Instead, I engaged with it on my own terms. I decided to fully *accept* my ego-mind *as is*. It's an integral part of who I am and always will be. Not only did I accept it, but I began to take responsibility for my ego-mind. This meant I had a role in managing it in the future.

The next thing I did was to give my ego-mind a new name. I called it "little-me." I reviewed what it was innately good at: recalling facts, accessing skills, learning, and applying knowledge. Tasks of writing reports, researching ideas, operating my car, and keeping records were suitable little-me projects.

This is how I began to reorient my mental priorities. In a way, it reminded me of how I used to supervise employees in the workplace. Often it took some tinkering to get people into the roles they were best suited for. This became my approach toward little-me.

A new normal was emerging in my life based in right thinking and appropriate action. I remained alert to what my mind focused on. When fear or resistance kicked in, I taught myself to relax while I looked into the situation more closely. I continued to call on little-me to gather and evaluate data as needed to make choices.

But *meditation* became the place where I brought important decisions to be finalized. Stillness had a way of helping me sense the right course of action. I gave myself plenty of time to "feel" the direction to take. I learned to trust the responses because they emerged—not from little-me—from my soul.

LITTLE-ME UNDER STRESS

If you've relied too much on little-me in the past, it's time for your soul to have a say. Use the tools at hand to manage little-me appropriately. When little-me is given the jobs it excels at, overall you'll feel more peaceful.

How little-me reacts to stressful situations doesn't have to be automatic. Obviously, in an emergency, you'll take appropriate steps without delay. But in day-to-day conflict situations, you can mentally take a step back. Get enough distance to observe what's really happening. In the beginning, your habitual stress response may kick in with a surge of adrenaline. You can learn to recognize this and make a new choice.

Relax your body as much as possible and breathe deeply. Inhaling and exhaling rhythmically, you can focus on your breath just as in meditation. We're talking about seconds here, not a long time. In your mind or out loud, you can call on the words of the mystic Julian of Norwich, "All is well. All is well." Do this even when things are *not* going very well at all, according to little-me.

Your experience with stillness can help to prevent a slough of negative emotions from unleashing. Ask yourself: "What is most important here—for me to get upset or maintain my peace of mind?" For much of my life, I didn't value peace of mind—because I didn't know it was even possible. If this seems familiar to you, know that there's hope for change.

In an upset state, our energy contracts and the field of possibilities narrows. Pursuing calmness in an otherwise agitating circumstance represents a profound change. It allows us to open to the bigger possibilities of the moment.

Where does taking action fit in? We hold off until we feel centered inside. Pausing in this way doesn't mean that we're doormats. Rather, we stand in a position of strength by taking the time to calmly assess our response.

In a conflict, you can signal the other person that you'll be taking time to think about what's just happened. This is a perfectly reasonable response. It gives you room to thoughtfully consider your next action. Few of us can think clearly on our feet in a heated situation.

During this time of reflection, little-me will likely have an opinion about what should be happening. Remember that it wants to be right or at least to defend itself. Even now, my own little-me snaps to it sometimes before I can collect myself. Far from being perfect at maintaining my calm, I keep a ready store of humor and humility close at hand.

<hr>

～～ GUIDED PRACTICE ～～

Little-me is often a reactionary. It can get you worked up in a split second with its fear-based approach. Spend time observing little-me, just as you did with your expectations. This exercise is one step toward managing little-me.

Let's examine how you respond during stressful events. When one occurs, remain as calm as you can in order to notice your otherwise-habitual response. Observe yourself, the people around you, and the developing incident with detachment. Do something only when you feel an inner centeredness. Often, there will be no immediate action that you really need to take. Make notes in your journal after several days of practice.

- ✦ What situations spark an immediate reactionary response from you?
- ✦ What self-talk or inner prompt allows you to separate from little-me in tense moments?
- ✦ How are you learning to manage little-me?
- ✦ What else is revealing the progress you're making?

SERVING SOUL

Amazing things can happen when a poet's genius is taken to heart. "Gotta Serve Somebody" guided me to whom I'll serve from now on. My unwavering choice is to serve my soul. This fulfills my desires for how I show up in the world and connect with Spirit.

We're called to place our fullest attention on soul as our ultimate guide. By focusing this way—and using our mind properly—we come to know cohesiveness and balance. Welcome to living a soul-filled life!

─☙ *Milestone* ☙─

The journey of soul is one of deepening trust with the divine and self. You are giving yourself over to the unseen—something your mind may be unsure about. But your heart knows you're on the right path, always moving in the direction of wholeness.

Spiritual life is a balance between the solitary and the communal. It's likely that you've had several pivot points of growth recently. This could be a good time to look for like-minded people to share your progress with. Spiritual companions can offer a space for deep insights, joyful celebrations, and meaningful support.

A new confidence is arising in you. Your intuition is stronger. Life is richer and more satisfying because your soul is finally having the chance to express itself. You glimpse what it is to have a mighty soul and be a mighty soul. Embrace the truth of who you are by saying out loud:

I am a mighty soul.

In your journal, reflect on these questions:

- How do you feel about the idea of being a mighty soul?
- How could this identity alter the way you show up in the world?

WITHIN MAN IS THE SOUL
OF THE WHOLE; THE WISE SILENCE;
THE UNIVERSAL BEAUTY, TO WHICH
EVERY PART AND PARTICLE IS
EQUALLY RELATED,
THE ETERNAL ONE.

Ralph Waldo Emerson

Your Mighty Soul

THE REINS OF OUR LIFE have been handed over to the care of our soul. We're beginning to know peace. Emotional ups and downs will still occur depending on our reactions and responses to our circumstances. But a good portion of the time, we'll find life to be balanced and even. Bravo!

Our inner architecture more closely reflects our divine nature now. Early on, we made a commitment to waking up spiritually. This is a choice to be renewed each day. When we aren't mindful or become tuned out, the difference is apparent. It's time to ask, "In what ways can I be more conscious today?" or "How can I wake up more fully?"

Over time, wakefulness becomes more of a natural state. This brings to mind a widely circulated tale about the Buddha.

> On the road one day, a Brahman priest observed Buddha's radiant presence. He asked, "Master, are you a god?"
> "No," Buddha replied, "I am not a god."

"Are you a magician or wizard?"

"No," Buddha answered, "I am not a magician or wizard."

"Are you a man?"

"No, I am not a man," he said.

"Then what kind of being are you?"

"Remember me, Brahman, as awakened."

In some versions, Buddha's final reply was

"I am awake."

Little-me tends to say that we're separate from everything else. Society reinforces this notion with its labels and categories. Buddha refused to be associated with anything but his awakened state. I don't know if the story I've shared really happened, but it epitomizes our own quest to stay awake spiritually.

Awakening is always a work in progress. Stillness has become our ready companion. More and more often, we use our mind appropriately. This helps us to stay in the present moment. We've jettisoned many preconceived filters, which leaves us with healthy curiosity, thoughtful questions, and many fewer assumptions.

Struggles will arise now and then as they have throughout our life. When interpersonal dramas make the occasional appearance, little-me may have gotten on first base. The good news is that we know how to manage this now: Step back, let go, and refocus inwardly.

You and I have been fellow travelers on a road with twists and turns. We've come to learn the importance of *abiding*, a word we don't hear often. To abide means to remain with or patiently wait for something. We realize that things around us develop in an organic way. There's no need to rush or force. By listening to our souls, we'll know what to put our attention on and at what pace, when to speak and when to remain quiet.

We feel thankful for the fertile and abundant universe we live in. The uncertainties of little-me have been supplanted by feelings of wonder and gratitude. We honor our aliveness and all the miracles of sight, sound, and touch.

Now I'll describe five attributes which mighty souls will know and experience to different degrees. These characteristics can and will enrich your life beyond measure.

AWARENESS

Awareness is the hallmark of an awakened life. When you're spiritually aware, you are receptive to or possess wisdom about something. Awareness can be a felt sense or a knowing in the mind—or both. Intuition is one aspect of awareness. You can think of it as being alert, alive, conscious, sensing, and mindful all at the same time.

Our ability to be self-aware and outwardly aware allows us to embrace a greater playing field in life. When opportunities arise in our personal landscape, we can see them more clearly. Additional details and relationship nuances come into focus. We're flexible in responding to situations—knowing that little-me's "one size" reaction doesn't fit all.

Let's look at how awareness can guide us through a common workplace challenge. I hear from many people who are facing workplace reorganizations. They're experiencing revised roles, new supervisors, uncertain expectations, and high stress. In a major change event such as this, awareness connects us to our source of personal power.

Right away we know to redirect little-me from its automatic fear reaction. Getting out of fear is the best thing we can do. Using the wisdom of our souls, we seek an overall "read" of the situation. This gives us a perspective on the company and perhaps our place in it. Awareness can also help us pick up cues from new bosses. We can see different avenues for building rapport. Our predominant emotion is compassion for everybody involved.

We take questions with us into our daily meditation time, such as: "Is my job in jeopardy?" "Is it best for all concerned if I look for another position?" "How can I be more useful in this situation?" and "Where do I most need to be mindful?"

Because of our heightened awareness, impressions come to us that may signal the next step to take. Inner calmness allows us to interpret signs and symbols correctly. When no answers come forward, we remain patiently in place and do the job that's in front us. Perceiving job reorganization as *practice* for a soulful way of being can be a helpful way to view it.

As mighty souls, we've developed a set of disciplines that reinforce our emerging awareness. These approaches help keep us on the spiritual path. One of our disciplines is to closely monitor our mind. We keep it focused on its best tasks. Other disciplines include stillness, reflection, and openness to guidance.

We embrace discipline when we're fully committed to a particular outcome. Attention to the soul is a high priority for us now. We're willing to pay the price of admission with our time and energy. While our day job is still there, loved ones deserve attention, and bills must be paid, we make time daily to inquire: "Am I feeling at one with my soul? Or have I wandered into little-me territory? How is my stillness practice going?"

Awareness shows up in small and big ways. It can be as simple as holding the door for someone behind you as you go into the post office. Or as deep as being led to say or do something that makes a huge, positive difference. You'll notice these events of awareness when they occur. It's good to acknowledge them as gifts.

Oftentimes, awareness serves to drop the barriers between people. It nudges us to give up judgments, expectations, and whatever else separates us from others. A recent incident brought this aspect of awareness home to me.

I was busily writing when the fire truck came onto our street, siren blaring. Glancing out a front window, I saw two cars at awkward angles in front of our property. The fire truck parked behind one of them, an arriving ambulance stopped behind the other. Dreading a wreck scene, I walked through our heavily treed front yard toward the gathering of people and vehicles.

A man was lying in our ditch, facing away from me. It took a moment for me to recognize him as our elderly neighbor, I'll call him Donny, who lives with his aged parents. My husband and I know him by name and wave when we see him walk by. Nearly every day he joins his friends at the convenience store to drink beer. Sometimes we've seen him staggering home.

One of the firemen remarked to me that Donny couldn't get up. I stood out of the way, thinking I might offer information to the EMTs at some point. Mostly, I just hoped Donny would be all right. One of his brothers walked over. I recognized him by the cowboy hat he always wears. He looked down at his prone sibling, then rolled his eyes. For a couple of minutes, he was silent and paced back and forth, avoiding eye contact with any of us. Then I watched him mumble Donny's name to a tech in charge and leave before the gurney was loaded.

My role that day was one of observer. I witnessed a person who'd stumbled and couldn't right himself. I saw Good Samaritans aid a stranger by blocking traffic with their cars. I looked on as medical professionals performed their rescue with compassion and efficiency. And I noticed a family member who judged and abandoned.

Awareness had allowed me to stand by without judging Donny, his alcohol, or the brother's behavior. It surprised me to discover a part of myself in *everyone* I saw. During my life, I've been a person who lost my footing and someone who aided others selflessly. I've also walked away in disgust from a family member. My sense is that God wants us to have affinity with each other. Oftentimes, awareness is how this happens.

～～～ GUIDED PRACTICE ～～～

For your journal work:

+ What instances of heightened awareness have you noticed within the past two weeks?
+ Do you feel a greater sensing and/or inner knowing? If so, how has this altered your responses to situations?

SURRENDER

Surrender is the act of yielding to divine grace. This is altogether like the acceptance work we did during our life review. Remember how freeing it was to let go of things from the past? A huge burden comes off our shoulders when we give up control.

Surrender is the process of letting go. If you learned to swim, you may've practiced floating on your back in the water.

Lifting your feet off the solid bottom and leaning way back was scary at first. Yet the water buoyed you up, didn't it? Surrender is like that. Something bigger carries you, and in time you have confidence in it.

It's a comfort to know that our intellect remains intact when we surrender. We don't have to give up who we are as individuals. Our same preferences and desires, goals and dreams, are there, along with our quirks and even our endearing habits. Underneath it all, there's divine support for us as we move through life.

Surrender involves a complete dependency on God for our ultimate care. This realization is an important aspect of waking up spiritually. Unlike other dependencies we may've known, surrender is based in *humility* and *trust*.

My definition of a humble person is someone who is authentic and open. While she might have healthy pride at accomplishing something personally meaningful, her feelings are infused with deep gratitude. The root word of humility is *humus*, meaning ground. The attitude of humility is groundedness. It's not low or subservient, but rather straightforward, modest, and inclusive.

Humility reveals a more mature understanding. A humble person realizes that he isn't God and doesn't see the entire picture. He's receptive to divine guidance at all times and places. True humility fosters gentleness toward life. Resistance melts in the face of it, including little-me's penchant for being "right."

Speaking of little-me, there are still times when my little-me tries to take control of a situation. It has become fearful over something and grabs my attention. I'll suffer with the problem for a while until I get my wits about me again. Then I hand the situation back to Spirit for resolution.

Humility helps us to give up judgments and opinions about what other people should or shouldn't think or do. We don't spend time trying to change others. Our role is to not interfere unless asked directly for help. Surrender acknowledges that God is in charge of everybody.

That said, sometimes I find myself in conversations with friends and acquaintances where it seems useful to point out something. If I feel led to mention an idea, I will. Humility brings us a different job than before. "Ambassadors of goodwill"—that's who we are now. We love and affirm the people who come into our lives. Grace enters the sacred spaces we've made possible through our surrender.

To surrender is to trust in the power of goodness. We rely on the divine hand to be at work in every situation, not just the ones we can easily turn over to Spirit. We give up depending on our individual mind to figure out life. This is one of the most liberating aspects of living from soul. All of us have tortured ourselves with *why* questions. "Why did the young mother die and the old man live so long?"

Through surrender, our insatiable *why* questions transform into something quite remarkable: the acceptance of life as *mystery*. We're free to be as curious about everything as we want, learning as much as we can our whole lives. At the heart of it all, however, we embrace the mystery.

On television and in books, mysteries intrigue us. We want them to be solved in good order, though. In life, the answers to mysteries may come months or years later—or not at all. Accepting and trusting this aspect of existence is one of our challenges. Perhaps not surprisingly, one of the names given to God has been Unknowable Mystery.

About ten years ago, I had a personal brush with divine mystery:

> I had pulled onto the right lane of a three-lane freeway at evening rush hour. I didn't misjudge the situation; I'd checked twice to see that I could merge safely. However, a woman in the middle lane driving a black Ford pickup, just in front of my car, moved into my lane without looking—at seventy-five miles an hour. I know, because I kept an eye on her vehicle as I accelerated. She never looked over to see that the front of my car was in the roadway.
>
> I remember thinking, "This is it. This is how my life ends." There was no time to feel afraid, although for a millisecond I wondered if it would hurt a lot to die this way. Expecting to feel metal crashing around me, the next moment came as a total surprise. My car was on the shoulder of the highway, coasting along at about thirty miles per hour. I had no awareness of how

it got there. Physically, it didn't seem possible. I know that I didn't drive the car there.

I recovered my composure enough to offer thanks and head home. I kissed my husband when he arrived from work and told him of my certainty that one of God's angels had surely been a veteran NASCAR driver.

Why I was rescued from dying on the highway is a mystery to me. I don't speculate much about it. I'm too busy entrusting my life to Spirit's direction.

~~~~~ GUIDED PRACTICE ~~~~~

For journal reflection:

+ In what ways have you found yourself in a state of surrender to the divine?
+ What did you let go of in order to do this?
+ What's different now?

RADICAL LISTENING

The language of soul speaks in stillness. To hear it is to become a *radical listener*. The word radical has multiple meanings, and one aspect relates to root or source. To listen radically is to receive guidance via the soul from the source of all, God.

Regular meditation helps us to listen intentionally at the deep levels needed. Soulful eyes and ears allow us to observe things more closely. A rich world full of insights and shifts in perspective opens to us. Here's an experience of radical listening that I had eight years ago.

> *A friend of mine who lived in another city had developed cancer. Each week I sat in stillness to send loving, healing energy and light to him. The first time I did it, my prayer wasn't quite finished before I distinctly heard these two words in my mind: Trust God. It was as though someone had spoken them directly to me. The same thing happened the next time I sat down to pray. I shared what I'd heard with one of his family members. Both of us were very moved.*
>
> *As you might imagine, I made sure to focus on trusting God for my friend's care during his illness and eventual passing. Although I didn't get what I "wanted," which was his survival, my gift of radical listening was the strong current of love I felt between us.*

When we initiate radical listening ourselves, the process can have three stages: (1) an asking-inquiry step, followed by (2) deep attentiveness, and (3) an identified action to be taken, if any. All three are important; none of them should be rushed or skipped. We start by taking time to formulate an open-ended question. Then we sit with the question in quietness and receptivity. Finally, an action step may come to us, or it may not. We trust the process and ourselves.

Mighty souls are discerning listeners. Yet that doesn't mean we're immune from the dulling effects of certain common activities that may block our ability to listen.

Television, news, sports or celebrity worship, social media and gaming, even fitness regimens can be tremendous distractions when not managed properly. Lulled to "sleep" by these attractive packages, our inner awareness can drop by the wayside. If this is your situation, use the ways you've learned to redirect your attention. You can make a choice to limit your time spent on those activities.

Another pitfall has to do with focusing too much on negative events. Media reporting of local and global tragedies, such as plane crashes, shootings, floods, and wars, can be over-the-top. Viewing endless tape replays and news commentaries is detrimental after a while. It drains us when we become enmeshed in things outside of our control.

Mighty souls are sensitive listeners, so it's important to take breaks from television during a crisis. During our stillness times, we can focus on accepting what has happened and send healing prayers.

Feeling compassion about tragedies and losses is a good thing. It demonstrates our keen awareness of the suffering of others. Compassion can have an active component to it also.

We might hear or sense a nudge to volunteer our time, donate cash or property, or simply offer more prayers.

When we listen to and act upon any guidance offered, there's a sense of peace and balance within us. Thoughts are constructive rather than fearful. We can become more fully present during a crisis, which allows us to help others.

As a radical listener, your job is to attend to the ways the soul expresses itself. Outward signs, inner knowing, dreams, visions, and the occasional voice in the head (like I heard) can all be valid communications. What matters is that you're aware of receiving a message, and you pay attention to what that message might mean for you.

Mystical experiences may occur more frequently as your receptiveness increases. If this is a new experience for you, it could be disconcerting at first. You can look to the Bible and other spiritual texts for a hundred examples of how God and angels have interacted with people in these same ways. The mystical visions I've had have been positive experiences. If they hadn't been, you can be sure I'd sit down with a professional counselor.

I'll share one of my earliest mystical experiences. I'd been especially low in spirits; some folks label times like this the "dark night of the soul." Only, for me, it had been weeks long.

> *I turned out my bedroom light about 11 p.m. to go to sleep. Suddenly, I found myself across the room on my couch.*

Everything else looked normal in the dim room. Some move-
ment above me caught my eye. It was a small blob of light with
soft edges. Within a few seconds, it turned into a white dove.
The bird looked at me serenely as it mostly floated, occasionally
flapping its wings.

As it made a lap around the room, the thought came (more
to my heart than my head) that this bird was an aspect of God,
the Holy Spirit perhaps, demonstrating Its eternal presence to
me. The image dissolved gradually, and I found myself back in
bed. The clock showed 11:10.

This vision helped to lift me out of my spiritual doldrums.
I'd been looking for answers, and doves have a rich, symbolic
meaning in Christian tradition. I felt renewed hope, encouragement, and aliveness from this experience. Afterwards, I was able
to take more active charge of my mind.

Radical listening can take you places you never thought
you'd go. Not every interaction with the divine will make
sense logically. Yet it's part of the magic and beauty of a soul-
filled life.

~~~~~ GUIDED PRACTICE ~~~~~

For journal reflection:

+ How has the quality of your listening at a deep level changed along your journey?
+ In what ways have you received soul communications?
+ How did you sense that the messages were indeed sourced in soul?

TRANSFORMED RELATIONSHIPS

In every relationship, we choose how much of ourselves to reveal. Partnering with the divine enables us to gradually lay down our lifelong armor. Relationships can blossom as our true, soulful nature steps forward. There's opportunity for real intimacy in our friendships and family relationships.

Others sense these changes in us and draw closer. Because we don't superimpose expectations on people, they feel more accepted. Overall, healthier and more genuine relationships show up. At the same time, a few relationships, even long-term ones, may fade away. Some of these folks may not want to relate in deeper ways. New connections will emerge that match your growing interests—you can count on it.

Mighty souls know about the impact of individual behavior. We're aware that our thoughts and actions affect the larger whole. How we behave outwardly is like a boomerang coming back to land at our own feet. In allowing the soul to lead, we are sure to be a source of positive energy.

We know that God is everywhere, in all circumstances and all persons. Yet, everyone is capable of making poor choices at times, whether from ignorance or being "asleep." When we encounter this behavior in daily life, how we respond is based on inner guidance. Let's look at a couple of examples.

I once went to breakfast with Tim, a consultant friend. The diner was crowded, and our server didn't come by for more than fifteen minutes. We had a schedule to meet, so being ignored this way was disconcerting. It would've been easy for me to take it personally. When she finally approached our table, she was verbally short with us. We could've gotten upset or walked out. Instead we kept calm, sipped our water, and waited.

At her next stop by our table, Tim asked her about her day—how she must've already had some challenges and how it was barely 7:15. His demeanor was kind and understanding as he looked into her eyes. I watched her face soften immediately. Hand on her hip, she said, "Honey, you wouldn't believe. It started when I went out at 4:30 to come to work and had a flat tire . . ."

Our conversation was brief, and she got back to work. But those few moments of authentic connection clearly helped her to relax. We enjoyed our meal and her now-smiling service. Even her gait had changed. Beyond the price of the food, it cost Tim and me nothing but a generous attitude toward someone who was obviously struggling.

When we're dealing with a stranger like this, there's not much at stake. However, conflicts with co-workers, friends, or family members have long-term consequences. This greater risk calls for our soul to be the one in charge (not little-me, whom we know wants to be right and gets defensive). Having a brief mental checklist can help us judge if our mind is calm, our body is relaxed, and we've reflected on the situation before taking action. Even when soul is in the driver's seat, the relationship may turn out differently than we hoped.

Four years ago, my husband and I had an unexpected conflict with a family member with whom we also had business ties. During the interaction, he bullied and shouted that his position was the only correct one. After a short while, we told him the conversation was over and left the meeting.

This conflict blindsided my husband and me. We'd had such high hopes about the collaboration. It also revealed one of my expectations: how family members should act. I had to let go of that expectation in order to regain my peace.

> *After reflecting soulfully on the situation, my husband and*
> *I decided to sever the working relationship. I began to focus on*
> *wholeness for each one of us during morning meditations. My*
> *husband and I have forgiven him, ourselves, and the whole*
> *situation. The three of us can speak comfortably at family gath-*
> *erings now. While the relationship isn't what we'd anticipated,*
> *it's the best it can be.*

This is a close-to-home example of how not every relation-ship can be "fixed." Many relationships can be mended, but *all* of the parties involved must be capable and willing. Soul calls us to have boundaries with others. By reflecting on the guidance we receive, we'll know what boundaries to put in place.

In another type of circumstance, we might be able to com-municate our way through the conflict. Initiating a respectful conversation with the other party is the first step. Our intent would be to regain balance and peacefulness. We may or may not feel better about the overall situation, but we remain open to the best possible outcome.

Relationships will continue to be learning opportunities. And with soul at the forefront, personal relationships are some of our most marvelous gifts.

~~~~~~ **GUIDED PRACTICE** ~~~~~~

For journal reflection:

+ What tools do you have now for building closer personal relationships?
+ Identify a recent interaction where you applied soulful personal boundaries.

STATES OF BEING

Mighty souls find that they enter *pure states of being* more readily. States of being reflect our divine nature and the inner experience of being alive. These states aren't tied to particular circumstances or conditions—they emanate from our soul.

Joy, freedom, and love are three states of being that show how far we've come from a world managed by little-me.

Joy. Ancient Sanskrit writings refer to God as Pure Bliss, the thought of which takes my breath away. In the New Testament, joy is identified as one of the fruits of the Holy Spirit. Similarly, the thirteenth-century Persian poet and Islamic scholar Rumi wrote about how when you act from your soul, it's as though a river of joy moves in you. That's the best description of living from soul that I've seen.

The word joy in our culture has long been associated with the emotion of happiness. Actually, joy describes an inner state of delight, gladness, and yes, bliss. I believe that this is the way we're intended to live. Our wakeful journey begins to uncover it.

There's a deep contentment when we access the state of joy within us. We see the beauty and rightness around us. *All is well.* Yet there's also an edge to joy, a sense of anticipation, vibrancy, and aliveness. Our wild nature is set free. We can be spontaneous, sensual, hilarious, and maybe even outrageous!

Children readily express their natural joy, especially when they're at play. A child's imagination makes the world a magical place. Nothing is overly serious. He learns about being flexible while building a city of blocks and then knocking it down. There is a lightness and ease within him.

Living soulfully helps us hold things more lightly in the way children do. We rekindle our sense of humor and playfulness. Your own joy can be celebrated by singing songs in full voice while no one's listening. Smiling with your whole body. Dancing. Being silly. Laughing. Observing a rose in full bloom.

Children demonstrate another thing to us, which is the way of the beginner. Beginners don't have all the answers. Every day they learn something. They don't linger over mistakes but simply start anew. Being a joy-filled beginner for the rest of our days is one of the gifts of this way of life.

A mighty soul's inheritance is joy. Joy is here now. Feel the joy within. Be open to the surprise of it. Expressing your innate joy is *always* a possibility.

FREEDOM. Other than in political or security discussions, we don't talk much about freedom. It's important to know that *freedom is always an inside job*. When our empowered soul runs our life, and our mind contributes in a proper way, we are *free*.

Every person has the potential to experience authentic freedom. It's a matter of personal readiness. Over time, we accept that in God there's no separation. Our individual uniqueness is fully supported. The journey to freedom is becoming *more* of who we truly are, not less.

Freedom brings with it a lasting inner calm. Our days are filled with mostly positive thoughts. Feeling bad or having anxiety or anger is a sign that little-me has a toehold. If this happens, you can open an inquiry in your journal. When you feel unfree about anything, bring yourself into stillness and ask questions. See what draws your attention and follow those strands until an assumption, belief, or expectation shows up. It may be time for you to develop a new attitude or behavior.

Our soul nourishes the sense of personal freedom. We feel expansive inside, liberated from self-imposed bonds. We are bold and yet balanced. Possibility and hope and creativity flow. Our self-expression comes alive!

LOVE. Love is the essence of God and of you and me. People say that love never ends, and we can believe this. It's not confined to any spot or excluded from any place. Love pours out on everything and everyone like a gentle rain shower. By tuning in, we can feel the energy of this love in us and around us.

Love is a powerful, creative force. In many different forms, we've heard the same message: *Love is all there is.* Love carries us in its goodness through the best and worst of times. We remember this when we awaken in the morning, during the day, and before falling asleep.

The distinction between giving and receiving blurs in this state of love. Everything feels like a gift. Having self-love is a foundation of our well-being. It allows us to accept who we are, imperfections and all. We actually like the person we see.

Loving others and loving God are the most natural things in the world. A soul-driven life is a big-hearted life. We express love at every opportunity, a thousand times a week. It's as continuous as breathing in and breathing out. Love is all there is.

In growing closer to our true selves, we've grown closer to God. We begin to feel the universal love that existed in the beginning and never ends. Moving with complete freedom, love encircles everyone and everything. Its essence soaks in, and life arises from that place. Love feels beautifully familiar. You remember it now, don't you?

~~~~~~ **GUIDED PRACTICE** ~~~~~~

You can practice standing in joy, freedom, or love—each one of them is a great revitalizer. In a quiet moment, choose a sacred meditation spot as I did earlier in the book (e.g., a garden, meadow, cottage, or mountaintop). Go there in your mind. Breathe and relax as you stand in that space. Attune your senses and begin to feel everything around you. All that you smell, taste, touch, hear, and see becomes a part of you. Keep breathing rhythmically, allowing any random thoughts to pass on through.

Now you can call upon joy, freedom, or love to be with you in your sacred place. Imagine that your chosen state of being appears in front of you as a ball of light about the size of a softball. You can hold it in your cupped hands and observe it. After a few moments, see if it wants to expand. If so, let it fill your body and radiate several feet in every direction. Conclude by giving thanks for this experience. How do you feel?

Meditate on the following questions and be open to whatever you can remember. Write responses in your journal.

+ When in your life have you ever experienced exceptional moments of joy? Freedom? Love?
+ What did you notice during those times?
+ How did you feel afterwards?

- In what ways can you be in charge of your own experience in life?
- Ask yourself this question: "Who am I now?"

YOUR MIGHTY SOUL

Life is a journey of the soul, a path that always offers new and surprising gifts. You feel the joyful arms of the divine embracing you. Goodness and unconditional love flow in and through you. In accepting this, a peace beyond description settles over your life. There's no need to feel weak or unhappy ever again.

You are a mighty soul. It's your lasting identity. Your mind and heart and the very cells in your body now know the truth.

ABOUT THE AUTHOR

MOLLY GLENN writes and speaks on cultivating a deep and meaningful spiritual life. *Your Mighty Soul* is her first book. She's written articles and led workshops on spiritual growth. Molly shares her thoughts on soulful living at www.mollyglenn.com.

A self-described practical mystic, Molly has experienced firsthand the mystery and wonder of the divine. She invites us to get acquainted with our own souls. By following its guidance, we can learn to live authentically in joy and freedom.

Earlier in life, Molly had several diverse careers, including rancher/cowgirl, financial executive, public speaker, and college instructor. She holds a master's degree in interdisciplinary studies with a focus in communication and an undergraduate degree in business. Being a mom and grandmother are Molly's most cherished roles to date. She is married and lives close to the earth in central Texas.

Sacred Shore LLC

SACRED SHORE is a resource for deepening your relationship with God and self. Our publications and workshops promote wholeness and balance for body, mind, and spirit.

Spiritual growth for adults and children is our primary interest. Personal renewal can happen at any age. Our goal is to help people become more self-aware, authentic, and conscious in their daily lives.

Sharing the spiritual journey with others is a precious opportunity. Sacred Shore provides a safe place for relating in this way.

For information on our conferences and resources, visit
www.sacredshore.com.

Made in the USA
San Bernardino, CA
20 November 2016